The People's Histo

# Glimpses (
# Old South Shields

## A Collection of Photographs, Picture Postcards And Ephemera

by

### John Carlson and Joyce Carlson

A group of soldiers from the South Shields area. The date is believed to be just prior to World War One.

*Previous page*: The Market Square, *circa* 1900.

First published in 2001 by

The People's History Ltd
Suite 1
Byron House
Seaham Grange Business Park
Seaham
Co. Durham
SR7 0PY

ISBN 1 902527 27 5

# Contents

Introduction      5

Acknowledgements      6

1.   Fowler Street      7

2.   Ocean Road      17

3.   King Street      27

4.   The Market      39

5.   Views of South Shields      51

6.   People of South Shields      115

A military parade passing Ocean Road Congregational Church, *circa* 1900.

# Introduction

This book continues the loosely linked series of books, *South Shields Voices*, *The Peoples History: South Shields*, *Images of South Shields* and *South Shields Scrapbook* and as with the previous books there is no one dominant theme. However, we would guess the average age of the photographs is much older than previous volumes and they seemed more biased towards the town and its buildings rather than the people, hence the title *Glimpses Of Old South Shields*. We are particularly pleased to include images of main streets and shops.

At the time of writing a few of the town's more established traders such as Frank Lake in Fowler Street and Woods in Ocean Road have gone and there are campaigns running to save the old Smithy Tea-rooms adjacent to Kepple Street Bus Station and the Changes One record shop in Fowler Street. We hope they succeed but whatever the outcome we suspect there is source material there for future social historians.

If you have any photographs or stories about South Shields you wouldn't mind seeing in future editions of our books then the authors are contactable via the publisher's address.

A civil defence exercise in 1954. The map appears to be of the town. Second left is Libby Matthews.

# Acknowledgements

We are grateful to the following people for their help and advice:

Geordie Atkinson, Tony Austin, Dennis Boad, Keith Bardwell, Andrew Clark, Paulin Chiu, Mr & Mrs Horsman, Joyce Roberts, Mrs Bone, Flo Thorburn, Peter Headly, Roland 'Rolley' Headly, Frank Heywood, Doris Johnson, Paul Mabley, Neil Mortson, Cuthbert Nicholson, Kathleen Nicholson, Eddie Post, George Post, Stuart Smith, Robert Wray, Alan Packer, George Nairn, Cheryl D'or Ryan, David Barnsley, Paul Barrett, Ron Bell, Tom Best, Fred Bond, Kathleen Burdon, Ken Corner, David Charlton, Ron Davison, Thomas Dodds Johns, Harry Fitzsimmons, Irene Foster, Richard Fox, Mary Gibbs, John Gordon, Muriel Hanson, John Johnson, Derrick Knott, Justine Lenney, Joan Mullen, Eddie Post, Mr Purvis (The Pilot), Mary McNeaney, Alan Packer, Dallas Park, Irene Spence, Thelma Small (née Taws), Eva Todd, Neil Tweddell, Sheila Tweddell, Stan Tweddell, Robert Wray.

Additional photographs courtesy of South Tyneside Libraries, the Shields Gazette and Beamish, The North Of England Open Air Museum.

Some of the information on street names has been taken from *History in South Shields Street Names* by James Yeoman.

Charles Carlson in the backyard of 106 Broughton Road in 1958.

# FOWLER STREET

The instillation of the tramway junction between Fowler Street, Ocean Road, Mile End Road and King Street in 1905. At a time when walking was the main mode of getting about the town, all this muck and devastation being wrought by the council must have horrified many residents. As well as the digging up of the cobbles much of Fowler Street was being demolished to allow road widening for the tramway and the building of new and more impressive shops and offices. Some letter writers seemed to suggest that rather than demolition taking place to allow the building of the tramway, the tramway was being built to allow the council to get on with demolition and the rebuilding it wanted to do faster and on a large scale than would be otherwise possible.

An advertisement for J.H. Oliver Tobacconists, Fowler Street.

Passengers boarding a tramcar at the junction with Ocean Road, *circa* 1925. Oliver's is to the right.

South Shields Corporation Tramcar No 52 at the bottom of Fowler Street. While King Street and parts of Ocean Road and Mile End Road have lost much of their traffic, Fowler Street now seems to be the main bus route out of town.

Hopkinson and Brady Stationers, Booksellers and Circulating Library at 2 Albion Terrace Fowler, Street. The firm was established in 1900.

The exterior of the South Shields Gas Company's Fowler Street showroom, *circa* 1925.

The interior of the Gas Company's showroom. Again the date is *circa* 1925.

The 55 and $^1/_2$ Fowler Street premises of Messrs P. Jordon and Co Bedding Manufactures and Upholsterers. The business apparently catered to both domestic households and the furnishing of ships and owned a wholesale warehouse at No 5 Saville Street.

Fowler Street, *circa* 1900 before building work. We believe the camera would have been standing at what is today, 2001, just outside the entrance to the Denmark Centre. According to the historian Hodgson, around 1800 much of this area comprised of gardens.

The premises of Robert Rigby Cycle Agent and Athletic Outfitter located at 11a Albion Terrace, Fowler Street. The shop was established in 1900 and sold cycles such as Humbers, Swifts, Triumphs, Glorias, Royal Enfields and Ariels as well as being an agent for several makers of motor cars.

Fowler Street, *circa* 1938. This shows broadly the same area as the top image on the opposite page after the roadway had been widened for the electric tramway.

A.C. Wilkinson's, 'The Borough Hatter', 53 Fowler Street, *circa* 1900.

E. Thomas, Carver, Gilder, Fine Art Dealer, Moulding Importer, located at 85 Fowler Street. The firm also made Saracenic Fitments 'for cosy corners in drawing and dining rooms, verandas, etc.'

*Right and opposite page*: An aerial view of the top of Fowler Street, *circa* 1960 with the Town Hall clock tower just visible to the right.

What is believed to be snow clearance work at the top of Fowler Street, 1886.

The view from the top end of Fowler Street looking along Westoe Lane, *circa* 1900. The photographer is standing on what is now no longer just a road but a 'quality bus route'. This image is from a tinted postcard and it is possible some of the buildings in the centre have been doctored by the photographer. Otherwise many of the buildings are little different today. The traffic situation however, is considerably different.

Looking along Claypath Lane, 1938. The Britannia public house is on the right.

# OCEAN ROAD

A tramcar at the pier head, *circa* 1910. Behind that stands the Wouldhave Memorial and, just visible behind that, the structure housing the Tyne lifeboat. The authors understand that in 1936 this structure was moved several yards north to allow road widening. In 1960, Councillor A.F. Gompertz, who helped establish the South Shields Entertainment's and Publicity Committee condemned an event staged at the nearby Pier Pavilion. This was the attempt of a forty year old Manchester housewife to play the piano non stop for 132 hours, smashing the world record by one hour, which he said brought the pavilion down to the standards of a 'cheap Jack fairground show.' Promoter Mr Bernard Wooley said around four thousand people a day were paying to see Mrs Ashton play and that children were giving her gifts of sweets and cigarettes. Previously the Entertainment's Committee refused an application by the Pavilion manager to exhibit a girl in a bottle on the grounds that he had previously upset people with a mummy display at Rhyl.

The Figure of Eight Railway at the Pier Head. This area has long been the site of amusements in one form or another. In 1825 Mr George Potts, who later became an Alderman, revived the South Shields races on the sands. This event later drifted into the hands of publicans and the races seem to have became an occasion for riots and drunkenness. Hodgson notes that on Tuesday, 29th May 1855 shortly before midnight, the police, hearing a great disturbance in one of the drinking tents belonging to a Newcastle publican, entered and found a young man named Adams, who said that he had been knocked down by some Irishman, and that a deaf and dumb boy belonging to South Shields had been even more brutally treated than himself. In the tent were about forty Irishmen, including one Peter Campbell, a beer house keeper at North Shields, whom Adams accused of assaulting him with a bludgeon. Campbell made a rush for Police Constable Kidd, but was stopped by Sergeant Richardson, and a number of civilians joined in the fray. The whole body of Irishmen then attacked the police, using bludgeons and broken seats as weapons and drove the constables out of the tent. A reinforcement of police came up, but were attacked, and three constables – Mathieson, Hudson and Atkinson – badly injured. The rioters then fastened themselves in the tent, and on Superintendent Bridges arriving with the Mayor and demanding admission, a pistol was fired at him. The police however rushed the tent, a number of South Shields folk joined in the attack and a general melée ensured with order only being restored by arrival of strong reinforcements of the North Shields and River Tyne Police.

John Hull with his grandson Harry Mabley at the pier head, *circa* 1950.

South Shields Spa Roller Skating Rink. The rink was also the venue for dances, boxing matches and political meetings and it was here the world endurance roller skating record was broken by Mr Arnold Binns of Hebden Bridge, Yorkshire in 1931 who skated non stop for 72 hours and 18 minutes. In about an hour in January 1932 the rink burned down in what was described as an awe inspiring site, quickly being reduced to a few blazing stumps and charred boards. Three or four of the decorated pylons also survived along with the boiler house which remained intact. An eyewitness gave a graphic account of the fire. 'I was going to work and was at the top of Roman Road when I saw a terrific glow in the sky. When I reached Park Terrace the glare was reflected on house fronts and windows and there were sleepy eyed spectators up at every attic window. I reached the Spar, the place was a mass of flames and the figure eight railway was blazing at the top and I could see through the window to a roaring inferno inside. It was a terrifying yet spectacular sight. The flames were over 50 feet high and the glare was so bright that the front beams stood out black against the fire. The breeze was carrying the smoke out to sea.' Apart from the loss of the rink, which was owned by the corporation, also destroyed were about a thousand pairs of roller skates belonging to Skating Rinks (Great Britain) Ltd, and the private property of manager and musical director Fred Lucas which included his violin worth three figures. Total damage including the rink was estimated at £5,000. An event to be staged at the rink later in the week by the police benevolent fund was not surprisingly cancelled.

Ocean Road Post Office, *circa* 1901. It is believed the man in the doorway is proprietor John Lawson. The shop stocked fancy goods, purses, card cases, wallets, pocket books, glove, tie and handkerchief boxes, prayer books, prayers and hymnals in cases, birthday books, music cases, ladies companions, writing cases, while a novel lending library contained, 'some hundreds of volumes of the latest and freshest literature of today.'

Waud and Robinson, Grocers and Provision Merchants, 1901.

Ocean Road, *circa* 1958. Note the crowds of people staring in the gift shop windows.

The exterior of the British and Oriental Depot, *circa* 1900. We believe the British Oriental Depot was formed in 1899 and that there were later ownership connections with T&G Allan, the book and stationary company. After over sixty years

supplying goods and souvenirs to visitors and townspeople alike it closed its doors in 1963.

The Grand Electric Theatre. The building was destroyed by fire in 1932.

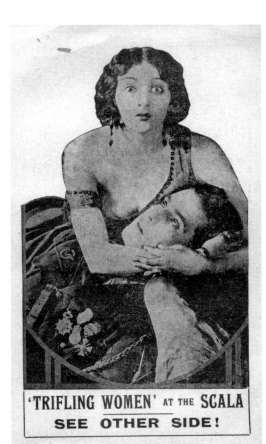

The front and back of a publicity card for *Trifling Women* shown at the Scala Cinema in South Shields in the 1920s. The film's leading lady, Barbara La Marr, started life in Richmond, Virginia, as Rheatha Watson. During her brief heyday in the early '20s, she starred in such costume epics as *The Three Musketeers* (1921) and *The Prisoner of Zenda* (1922). Described by the newspapers as 'the girl who was too beautiful', the exotic-looking star had a sunken onyx bathtub with gold fixtures installed in her mansion. Married four times, twice before going to Hollywood, she died in 1926 at the age of twenty-nine from a drug overdose that the press reported as 'overdieting'. In the 1930s the head of the MGM studios, Louis B. Mayer, used her surname for Austrian actress Hedy Kiesler. As Hedy Lamarr, she also starred in several films at the Scala.

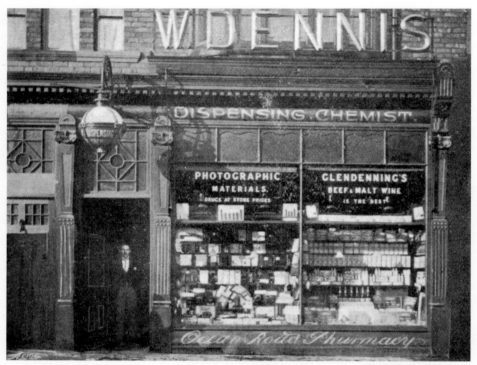

The exterior and interior of the Ocean Road Pharmacy and Dispensing Chemist, *circa* 1903. The proprietor was Mr W. Dennis MPS who sold all kinds of pharmaceutical goods as well as cameras, magic lanterns and slides.

A parade passes through Ocean Road, *circa* 1960. Curious trolleybus passengers stare down at a float on the theme of Noah's Ark.

Ocean Road, South Shields    7044

A Monarch postcard view of Ocean Road.

OCEAN ROAD, SOUTH SHIELDS (329)

A Monarch postcard view of Ocean Road from the end of King Street. Although there are many pedestrians about, there seems to be little traffic. The electric tramlines are in place suggesting this is at least 1906. The Criterion public house seems to selling itself to the public as a restaurant rather than simply a place to drink alcohol. It would be interesting to find a photograph of the inside of the dining area. In the latter years of the 19th century the rising number of visitors arriving to the town through the new railway station in Mile End Road helped Ocean Road prosper and fill out with very impressive looking shops and places of entertainment. Ocean Road runs along a natural depression which causes many people to think it was once an outlet of the River Tyne to the sea. Its position has meant that the area has long suffered problems with drainage. In the past the area has suffered from both a tendency to flood and problems in getting rid of sewerage. Around 1875, in a bid to alleviate these difficulties, a main sewer was constructed along Dean Street, Market Street, King Street and the full length of Ocean Road at a cost of £5,000. In 1900 this was extended across the then new South Park and by way of Bents Road to the then new districts around Mowbray Road. We believe that after the Second World War there were proposals to demolish the Criterion on the grounds that it was to old fashioned and replace it with a new building or even use the empty site to create a public square.

# KING STREET

A parade passes from King Street to Ocean Road, *circa* 1960.

An illustration of Hardy's Furniture Store, King Street, taken from a 1920s advertisement. The building still stands today and is used as the town's branch of the fast food outlet McDonald's. The vertical sign outside Hardy's was a feature in King Street for many years and can often be glimpsed on old photographs. Today this area is one of the most impressive parts of the town and we suspect most visitors who walk towards Ocean Road from the area of the Metro/Bus interchange will be impressed by buildings such as the old library and the former Marine School. By evening, and particularly on a Friday and Saturday night, this area is packed with people having a good time in the area's pubs and clubs. However, around two hundred years ago this area was very much on the outskirts of the then town centre. Hodgson notes that around 1800, King Street was a quaint thoroughfare, its buildings picturesque in their irregularity, many of the houses low with red tiles and high pitched roofs, some even with fruit trees in the gardens in front and nearly all with cellar kitchens and railings. There were few business premises in the street but several public houses. The old brew house whose site was later covered by the Theatre Royal was a famous hostelry. The Golden Lion hotel was the first hotel for the accommodation of travellers in the town, and for many years was in the occupation of the Oyston family, the first of whom came from West Auckland.

The exterior of Messrs James Kerr and Co Cash Drapers, Nos 38 and 39 King Street, *circa* 1901. The shop was lit with electric light and had handsome plate glass windows which showed off the stock of mantles, millinery, laces, gloves, haberdashery, underclothing, general drapery and dress making fabrics. The second floor was devoted to waiting and fitting rooms while the dressmaking workshops occupied the third.

King Street looking west, *circa* 1900.

The Bridge Hotel and Bridge Chambers, No 33 King Street and Queen Street. On Monday 17th November it was auctioned at the Golden Lion in King Street. The Bridge to the right is now part of South Shields Metro Station while the hotel's ground floor is now occupied by Mayfair newsagents and Caxton's shoe shop.

The National Provincial bank, King Street in 1891. The building is now occupied by H. Samuel and is still very recognisable today except most of the 'detail' seems to have been plastered over. However, the two 'thistle' motifs alongside the second floor windows are still visible. The roof of a very interesting looking building can be glimpsed to the right in the Salem Street area.

Wares. The original shop was apparently the first in the town to be lit by electricity.

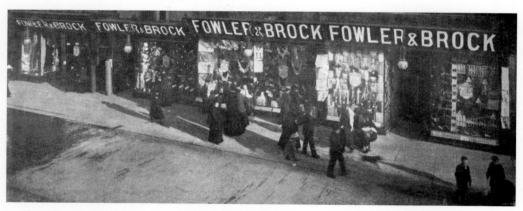

A shot from an unusual position of the windows of Fowler and Brock, *circa* 1901. The company began trading in Shields in 1892, describing their premises as striking, commodious and fitted with electric light. The shop was later taken over and developed into Binns.

# THE
# Tyneside Shopping Centre.

## LATEST FASHIONS at LOWEST PRICES.

Everything for Ladies' and Children's Wear.
RELIABLE HOUSEHOLD DRAPERY.

# FOWLER & BROCK, Ltd.,
## The Great Cash Drapers and Furnishers,
# KING STREET, SOUTH SHIELDS.

An advertisement for Fowler and Brock Ltd showing the King Street shop.

Grant's the Jewellers, *circa* 1905.

The interior of Grant and Sons, Clock and Watch Repair Workshop, 73 King Street. This is reputed to be all of the firm's staff of watchmakers gathered together.

A postcard view of King Street looking towards the Market, *circa* 1902.

King Street, *circa* 1910.

King Street, *circa* 1900. The buildings to the left are now the home of Marks and Spencer's.

Another postcard view of King Street taken either from or very near to the old Town Hall.

King Street, *circa* 1965.

King Street late 1999 with repaving work underway. The amount of time taken by this work and the level of disruption it caused was the subject of much comment in the *Shields Gazette*.

# *William Ernest Beck*

UNDER THE CLOCK.

*(Formerly MONCRIEFF & BECK)*,

Jeweller & Silversmith,

## 74, KING STREET,
## SOUTH SHIELDS.

"BEX"
Watches
can be
relied upon
for
Appearance.
Utility.
and
Economy.
Silver
English
Levers
from 32/6.

Acknowledged to be one of the Cheapest and Best Houses in the District for

### MARRIAGE GIFTS, PRESENTATIONS,

### CHRISTENING & BIRTHDAY GIFTS.

Large Choice of Silver and Electro Plate.    Exceptional Value.

Wedding, Betrothal, Diamond and other Gem Rings in great variety.

An advertisement for William Ernest Beck, Jewellers and Silversmiths, *circa* 1904.

# THE MARKET PLACE

A trolley bus laying over at the Market, 1954. Behind it to the right is the Market Hotel. Built in the 1870s the pub was demolished in 1965. Hidden behind the Market Hotel was the Nunnerie Inn. Visible to the rear of the bus is Beacon House, home to Barbour's Clothing Manufactures until they moved out in 1957. The Square's nature and character has changed much over time. It was the natural centre for trade and supplied the many ships drawn to the port of South Shields and by night it would be a drinking centre for these ships' crews who would fill its many pubs. Nowadays the centre of the town's nightlife has gravitated to the junctions of Fowler Street, King Street, Mile End Road and Ocean Road.

One of the earliest known photographs of Shields showing St Hilda's Church with the Market Square behind. According to Hodgson in 1768 the Dean and Chapter of Durham enclosed eight acres of land for the purpose of a market, having apparently induced the Curate of Saint Hild's, the Rev Samuel Dennis, to hand part of the Glebe land of Saint Hild in return for £30 per annum. Hodgson remarks that had the land remained with Saint Hilda's the church would soon have been one of the richest in the country. The area seems to have been chosen because it was reasonably central to the town while without directly intruding on the already congested main thoroughfares. The Dean and Chapter were also empowered by act of Parliament to lay out just over two acres of the land as a market square and surround it with associated houses, shops and warehouses. Under forty year building leases, much of this surrounding land later became East Street, West King Street, Thrift Street, Dean Street, West Street and Church Row. In the early 1800s burial space at St Hilda's Churchyard was running out and the overcrowded condition was seen as a public scandal. In 1805 the churchwardens advertised for about five acres of land for a new churchyard, apparently without result. The then Bishop suggested covering the churchyard with ships ballast to which there were objections regarding the necessary movement of graves. Around ten years later the authorities were driven to adopt the Bishop's suggestion using ballast from the highest hill around the Mill Dam. The work would also provide relief to men who were unemployed following reductions in the fleet and the army after Napoloen's defeat at Waterloo and a currency crisis that affected commerce and shipping. At a town meeting in December 1816 the suggestion was approved, a public subscription opened, and the unemployed of the town were engaged by the committee to carryout the work, the hours of labour being from 7.45 am to 4 pm with an hour's break for dinner.

Market Place, South Shields. 7046

A Monarch postcard of men gathered in the Market Place, *circa* 1905.

A description from September 1885 by an unnamed *Gazette* correspondent described the life of many of those who habituated the square around two decades earlier:

'It is a noticeable characteristic of modern communities that the sharp lines of division which separated men in the feudal times have disappeared, and that in our day one class or condition of men mergers into the next with graduations that are almost imperceptible. There are persons who are enormously rich and others who are abjectly poor, but between the social antipodes there are no clear lines of demarcation. Nowhere, perhaps, could this truth be more easily satisfied than the Market Place of South Shields. There, when the days are fine, do the citizens who are idle, either from choice or necessity, enjoy the companionship of their kind. On the outer segment of a circle whose centre is the Town Hall, the men of substance congregate in groups. Broadcloth, tall hats, ponderous watch chains and immaculate linen, are the outward and visible signs of easy circumstances. The talk here is political, commercial and speculative, the politicians alternating between the pavement and the petrified potatoes of the square, as the visits of the policemen may determine, discus the affairs of the nation with as much volubility as the average Briton is capable of.

The commercial men do not talk as much or linger so long, but there is a curious unanimity among both sections as to the place and purpose of adjournment. The sporting men are not much given to conversation, and their thoughts mainly appear to be recorded in a laborious fashion on the leaves of a dog eared book. 'Business first and pleasure afterwards' is the motto which finds most favour with the 'Bookie' and from early morning till the hour of the last race when times are good, he knows but little relaxation. The men who do business with him do not seem to consider it necessary to waste much time over the transaction. Near the centre of the circle 'box hats' are the exception and not the rule. Here and there linen is displaced by paper and the watch chains are not so numerous. The conversation is mostly retrospective and despondent, for these men are mechanics, who, for the lack of more profitable employment, assemble and meet together to recall with a sigh the days when work was plentiful and wages were high. There are some men who have had a fair share of employment in the past year, others, and they are by far the most numerous, have had none.

Close to the Town Hall and leaning against the pillars, or seated on the steps, are the men who have neither watch guards, collars, nor any other superfluities in the way of raiment. They are mostly of the class who do 'odd jobs'. A day or two at the shipyards, a few hours painting, or a job of 'striking' for a blacksmith – such are the irregular and often poorly paid devices by which the casual labourers digs out a joyless existence. There are men here who have learned and practised some handicraft, but 'the times are out of joint' and the craftsman is fain to do anything in an honest way which will supply a meal. The assembly here is motley and occasionally picturesque. Pacing the pavement in the shade during the summer days and on the lea side in winter are sailors, sun browned and muscular, but too often having the listless expression and eye that denotes hunger. These men have tired of sitting in the shed at Mill Dam and watching others as luckless as themselves flit out of the sunshine into the waiting room to gaze upon the board whereon the names of vessels taking on crews are now, but alas too seldom, recorded and then pass out again more despondent than before.

Occasionally we may see some dust stained vagrant halting on his pilgrimage to nowhere in particular, in a state of repose on the steps which leads to the halls of the high and mighty. Now and again some reveller full of whiskey and destitute of cash sleeps off the effects of his previous nights debauch with his head against the central column and his extremities bestowed at diver's angles. Hither also comes the loafer, firm believer in the doctrine that work was only meant for fools and horses. The function of the loafer is, of course, to loaf, and being fully aware of what is expected of him he fulfils his earthly mission as best he may. Through all the conversation of the men who gather in the Market Place there runs a saddening note. The views expressed about the coming winter are gloomy in the extreme. Last winter many working men, though unemployed, were able to stave off active want by the sale of their household effects, but that remedy is no longer available. Amongst the throng I have seen men who were most active in the work of relief during last winter, but who are themselves now out of employment. The works at the Lawe did much to minimise the suffering of the unemployed, as also did the various agencies so rapidly called into existence when the actual state of matters was made public. But according to the men the incoming winter will find as many unemployed, but with less resources than before. It is not my duty to comment on the statements that have been made. I simply set them down in order that, inquiry can be made and if needs be steps taken before the icy breath of winter has added the discomforts of cold to the pangs of hunger.'

S. 3306      ST. HILDA'S CHURCH AND MARKET, SOUTH SHIELDS.

A postcard view of St Hilda's Church and Market Stalls.

Prior to 1900 this area was considered for the site of a new Town Hall. The corporation obtained parliamentary powers for a new Town Hall building in 1861. There were suggestions that it should be located in the centre of the Square to form a covered Market Square at the south side. There was much public opposition to the idea of demolishing the old Town Hall. The North Shields artist Birket Foster RA said he and several of his friends of high artistic standing agreed that the building was in perfect harmony with the character of the town and that it was one of the moist satisfactory buildings in the North East. He also commented that the people of South Shields should have no business with the building of a 'Grand Gothic Town Hall' such as the one which had been built in Bradford. He concluded the old building, of whose merits familiarity has perhaps made the people less conscious than they ought to be, has great artistic merit, and to destroy it would be an act of vandalism which would certainly soon be regretted.

The Market Place, *circa* 1900.

On Thursday, 31st May 1888 under the direction of a Royal Commission inquiring into the working and management of markets and fairs in England and Scotland, Mr Cecil M. Chapman, barrister at law attended the Town Hall. The Town Clerk, Mr J.M. Moore explained that when the Corporation bought the Market and Fairs from the Dean and Chapter of Durham in 1855 the place was very rough and inconvenient for traffic and £1,600 was spent paving the Square and another £1,000 removing property near St Hilda's Church including the old vicarage. He then described the current state of the Square. A large business was done in terms of meat and in poultry both alive and dead. On Saturdays much business was done in merchandise. The undercover market under the Town Hall where local farmers could sell their poultry, eggs and butter had now fallen into disuse. No corn had been sold there for at least thirty five years. If demand necessitated, the Corporation would happily erect a covered market for the disposal of farm produce. Water was supplied to the stalls to help the sale of fish and this trade seemed to be growing to a large extent. Ald Donald said stall holders were charged 1 shilling for fifty square feet, which he thought was as low as it possibly could be, and four pence for the use of gas. He thought some of the stall holders took a considerable amount of money. The Commissioner asked if the stall holders ever requested that the market be covered and Ald Donald replied 'No, never.' A Mr Peacock said he was not well acquainted with market matters, but one or two of the stall holders had asked him to place one or two things before the inquiry. They would like to see full reports of income and expenditure each month and they objected to the Market Fund being mixed up with the Quay Fund. Mr Moore answered, 'That is not so!'

Mr Peacock resuming said they would also like to know why the Market was discontinued on a Wednesday. Mr Moore said they could have the Markets on a Wednesday if they liked or any other day of the week.

Mr Woolley said he objected to Ald Donald's remark that the stall holders made a considerable amount of money, but he could not say the charge for the stall was too large. He, however, objected to being turned off for the shows, which only came on Mondays, Fridays, Saturdays and Fair Times. Ald Donald said the shows had a right to stand there at fair times. At other times they got permission off the committee. They had granted Mr Woolley a concession of a particular corner.

PC Casting was then examined and also a man selling temperance drinks. The Commissioner asked if anyone could tell him the difference in price of articles sold in the Market and in the shops and Mr Woolley answered that it was ten or twenty percent. Mr Bowman said that that was where tradesmen with shops in the Market Place had reason to complain. A place in the Market Place cost one or two shillings from where £5 up to £30 worth of goods could be sold while shopkeepers were paying £80 or £90 a year for rent and rates and did less trade. The Commissioner said that the most eloquent fact that had emerged was that not a single person from the shop sellers to the stall holders made a complaint as to how the market was conducted.

The proceedings terminated and the members of the Council present and the commissioner partook of luncheon at the Royal Hotel, Ocean Road.

A group of market stalls at South Shields.

The Willie Wouldhave Public House. The building to the right still stands on what is now River Drive. One morning in March 1887 a coffin went on display inside one of the bars around the Market Place and a crowd of several hundred soon gathered outside. The coffin was pitch pine with brass mountings and on the breast plate were inscribed the words 'S.G. Fazzi born in London 8th February 1844. Died——.' It belonged to a Mr George Fazzi who intended to journey to London pushing his coffin before him on tricycle wheels. Mr Fazzi told the *Gazette*: 'I have wanted to go to London for these last seven or eight years but could not afford it. Therefore, I am determined to tramp to see the place where I was born. I am taking my coffin with me rather than anything else for the simple reason that if anything should happen to me on the way I shall not be chargeable to the parish. I leave three children. The eldest is a girl of seventeen years and the two younger, a boy and a girl will be in her charge.'

In the top of the coffin were two slits in which the money he expected to receive was to be dropped. While in the bar a number of coins were dropped in and were heard to rattle on the bottom of the coffin. At twelve o'clock Fazzi started on his journey, his progress along King Street attracting several thousands of sightseers. When he reached Sunderland the reception he received was to be described the next day by the *Gazette* as 'warm.' He was speedily surrounded by jeering men and lads took refuge in a public house in Monkwearmouth until after dark. About eight o'clock he attempted to quietly move his coffin to a beer house in Zetland Street, but again found himself surrounded. Stones and snowballs were pelted at him and he was obliged to appeal to the police for protection. Amid a tremendous hubbub he reached the beer house where his coffin was thrown over the back yard wall and damaged. He repaired it during the night and resumed his journey about eight o'clock the following morning. Almost as soon as he started a number of men threatened to pitch his 'machine' over Wearmouth Bridge and he was booed and pelted with missiles to the outskirts of the town. The *Gazette* commented that should he have many more similar experiences his coffin might be put to use sooner than he anticipated. Exactly why Mr Fazzi received such bad reception is not reported. However, he abandoned his journey shortly after leaving Sunderland.

The premises of James Mather and Co Wine Merchants, Dean Street. This street ran from the Market down to the Ferry Landing at the opposite side of the square to King Street. It still exists as a walkway although is now paved over and Wouldhave House now stands across its eastern end. The building to the left of this picture still stands however. Mather's building survived the bombing of the Second World War and the visit of a Zeppelin to the town in the first. It was demolished during the redevelopment of the square in the late 1950s and early 1960s. This is a shame as Mather was a great champion of the town, being a founder member of the Town Improvement Commission in 1829, and of many issues which concerned working and less well off people. He designed the first ships' lifeboat in 1826 and was heavily involved in the investigation of the St Hilda's pit

explosion in 1829 and also in pubic health issues. Indeed as one person remarked during work on this book his achievements had such positive ramifications for so many people world wide that South Shields could almost be marketed as James Mather Country if Catherine Cookson's appeal ever began to wear thin.

The Nunnerie Bar which was located behind Mather's premises in Dean Street. In the 19th century Shields seems to have had almost an overabundance of public houses. We believe that in 1834 publicans accounted for more than ten percent of the parliamentary electorate.

Corporation Tramcar No 23. From matching the stonework on the buildings behind up with other photographs we believe the car is on layover at the Market Square. It seems to be a cold, rainy day. The difference in attire between the conductor, who would spend at least some time inside the car and the driver who wouldn't, is striking. Curiously, the 'p' is missing from the Corporation on the car's side.

Corporation Trolleybus No 200 at the Market Square, *circa* 1960.

One of the town's shortest lived buildings, the City of Durham public house.
Built in 1938 by Truman's brewery, it was in rubble by 1941 being set on fire
by paint exploding from a nearby shop during the October air raids of that year.
It was rebuilt in 1961 on the site of the old market café and still stands today.

Trolleybuses around the Market Square, *circa* 1960. *Above*: At the east side of the Square with the entrance to King Street behind the rear bus. The old Tram Car Inn is visible to the right of the first bus. *Below*: A bus stands outside of Barbours premises on the west side of the Square.

# VIEWS OF
# SOUTH SHIELDS

Premises of Matthew Todd in Commercial Road, *circa* 1904. The nature of the business was described as Ship Store Merchant and dealer in Bond Stores.

Holy Trinity Church, *circa* 1900. High Shields Station is to the rear. Twenty three of the victims of the St Hilda Colliery disaster of Friday, 18th June 1839 were buried in the church yard the following Monday. Most victims were from the Templetown area. Hardly a house in the village escaped bereavement. Hodgson notes the victims interment was one of the most impressive spectacles ever witnesses in the Borough. A vast procession mustered in Templetown including thousands of miners from the surrounding collieries. Some of the coffins were placed in hearses but in many instances, where more than one victim had fallen in a family, two, three or even four were placed in a cart.

The North Eastern Railway Bridge over Laygate which formed part of High Shields Station. The Al Azhar Mosque now occupies the site of the buildings visible on the left behind the bridge.

View from under the bridge looking in the opposite direction towards Commercial Road which runs left to right at the rear of the picture. The high ground is being cleared of crumbling buildings. Hodgson notes the buildings had been erected on heaps of refuse from ancient saltpans including ashes, imperfectly consumed coal and waste salt and lime which was the cause of an underground fire which destroyed a meeting house in 1782. In February 1872 fire erupted underground, working its way slowly along Commercial Road destroying around twenty houses by 1876. It later spread towards Laygate and was not subdued until well into 1882.

What is now the Dolly Peel public house, Commercial Road. A section of the town's trolleybus overhead is visible. This photograph was taken by local photographer Tony Austin in April 1964 shortly after the trolleybus system had shut down.

W. Hay, Contractor for Chipping and Painting, Commercial Road.

The offices stables and yard of Messrs Hodge and Son, Haulage Contractors and Warehousemen, 15 Commercial Road, *circa* 1901. The firm, formerly known as Slaughter and Hodge, had a depository at the Market Place for the storage of dry goods such as pictures and pianos. They were also coal merchants, hay and corn dealers and were involved in the disposal of ships' ballast.

South Shields Corporation Tramcar No 26 at the foot of South Eldon Street, *circa* 1910. We believe the inspector is Robert Huntley and the area to the rear of the tram later became Greathead Street. No 26 was one of a series of ten cars, Nos 26-35, built for the Corporation in 1907 by the United Electric Car Company Preston. Livery was crimson lake and ivory with lining in gold.

Rebuilding work taking place on Stanhope Road School in 1936. The school had been damaged by a fire. At the front of the picture is Teddy Bennett, a labourer who lived in Oak Avenue.

A tobacconist and confectioners shop. The words 'Tyne Dock' are visible on the glass to the left although we are unsure of its precise location.

Corporation Trolleybus No 223 at the Tyne Dock terminus, September 1959. The buildings behind have since been demolished and the site used for road widening.

Tyne Dock.

A postcard view of Hudson Street, Tyne Dock. The old post office, which is still standing, is at the right. Part of the building was also used as a boys' club. Hudson Street is named after the 19th century 'railway king' George Hudson.

The premises of Messrs Walker and Darling Dispensing and Family Chemists, Hudson Street, Tyne Dock.

Buildings at the top end of Stanhope Road on the junction with Boldon Lane.
*Above*: Maynard's Newsagency. *Below*: A hardware shop. For many years this
has been a second hand shop and has traded under the name of 'Second Hand
Rose.'

Two photographs of North Eastern locomotives thought to be at Tyne Dock. The driver of the engines was John Thomas Horsman who was born in 1873. Sadly he died when he was in his fifties.

The Exchange Buildings,, Tyne Dock, *circa* 1901. They were located next to the then Tyne Dock Station. The three floor building was the premises of Messrs Adamson and Company, Oil, Paint and Ship's Store Merchants. Oil was stored in large tanks holding as much as 4,000 gallons. The building was also home to a large stock of paints, hardware, beef and pork in casks, butter, cheese margarine, tinned goods, tar and resin. The first floor contained the general offices for the firm. The top was utilised for the display of lamps, shades, cutlery, engine and deck stores.

Anthony Proud's Ship Engineering and Boiler Works, Tyne Dock. The business was established in 1869.

Dock Master's House, Tyne Dock. (424)

A Monarch postcard showing the Dock Master's house at Tyne Dock, *circa* 1905.

Hall Brothers' Timber Yards at Tyne Dock, one of the largest yards of its kind in the area. It was converted into a limited company in 1899 with Mr John Robertson as managing director. The Tyne dock premises had a river frontage of around a quarter of a mile and included moulding, sawing and planing mills. The creosoting works could treat timber such as telegraph poles up to 85 feet long.

The Coal Shipping Staiths, Tyne Dock, showing the South Eastern Gas Board collier *Chessington* loading coal for power stations in the South of England. When doors in the bottom of coal wagons on the staiths were opened the coal was fed down chutes into the hold of the colliers. 'Trimmers' levelled of the piles of coal to prevent it moving in rough weather, a dirty and dangerous job.

*North Devon* with *Iberian Coast* alongside, loading general cargo at the Sutherland Quay, Tyne Dock bound for Port Churchill, Hudson Bay Canada. The *North Devon* was taking part in the annual race to be the first vessel to birth in the port after the winter ice had thawed.

All Saints Church, Harton, Tyne Dock, *circa* 1905. Construction began on the church in 1887 at an estimated cost of £3,000. Of that £300 came from the Harton Coal Company. The consecration took place on 16th June 1890. The parish boundaries, formed in 1890, were defined by the then Sunderland Branch railway from the then boundary of Harton Township to the Boldon Lane crossing at Tyne Dock Station and then along the Pontop Branch Railway, roughly today's Metro, to the northern boundary of the West Park. Then south east to the old Borough boundary and across Harton Lane to the Harton Township boundary and back to the Sunderland Railway.

Vaux off licence at Francis Street, Tyne Dock.

Harton Colliery seen from the north. Believed to be May 1891 during rebuilding work.

A group of surveyors at Harton Colliery. Visible are a Level Miner's Dial and ranging pole. The date is believed to be around 1900.

A pit pony, 'Swallow', with driver and lads at Harton Colliery, 25th March 1912.

The stable yard, Harton Colliery, 1892

Workers at Harton Colliery. The dates of both photographs are believed to be early 1960s.

*Top image*: Cottages in Quality Row, West Harton. It was here that Wesleyan Methodists in the area started their own services around 1840 in a cottage then inhabited by a Methodist blacksmith named Richardson. Wesleyan Methodists had began in Harton during the early years of the 19th century. First meeting in a cottage at Harton Village near where the Vigilant pub is today, they later found more commodious quarters in the kitchen of James Urwin. It recalled that local preachers such as Joseph Reed and Henry Martin had a good time in the spacious kitchen. From Quality Row the West Harton Methodists later moved to Isaac's Court, (*Middle image*). Here the services were sometimes disturbed by the lower part of the premises use as a cow byre and the accommodation was so limited that Sunday School anniversary services needed to be held in the colliery joiners' shop. In 1863 they moved to what was usually know as 'The Old Chapel.' (*Bottom image.*)

A postcard view of the lake near the West Park.

The West Park Hotel, Stanhope Road. It was built in the 1890s on the outskirts of the town as accommodation for professional travellers. Residents apparently had a clear view of Cleadon water tower across the fields.

Members of Imeary Street Chapel Boys' Brigade outside the Chapel building in Imeary Street.

Imeary Street Chapel Boys' Brigade Sunday morning parade, 1934. Pictured from left to right are: L. Macy, S. Scott, J. Shelton, Wm Hedley and V. Ord.

The County, referred to in a 1901 guide as The County Hotel Family and Commercial. The guide refers to its proprietor as a Mr R. Henderson while the building itself was said to contain 'spacious and commodious coffee and commercial rooms; a very fine assembly room for banquets, weddings balls and capable of dining as many as a hundred and fifty persons at once; an excellent billiard room with table by Burrows and Watts; public smoke rooms; a well filed buffet bar; several quiet and comfortable private sitting rooms, bath-rooms, with all modern conveniences. There is a first class stabling and coach house accommodation, and the cricket and football fields, tennis ground, hockey and golf links, etc are close at hand.' The guide adds that the hotel is near the High Shields Railway Station, 'near' presumably being used in a very relative sense as we would estimate most other buildings in Shields would be as near to the station as The County.

A group of shops in Oxford Terrace, Westoe Road. We believe the shop to the left is now occupied by John Herring photographers while the two in the middle are now Farnsworth's Fruit Shop.

A Monarch postcard of Westoe Village. The type of tram in the background suggests the date is at least 1921. Note the horse trough to the right.

James Teasdale's shop in Imeary Street, one of the first motor dealers in the North East, *circa* 1915. On the left is James Teasdale Jnr with his sister Ethel. The firm was taken over by Adams & Gibbons around 1922.

Three images of Rosarium, one of the town's larger houses located on Sunderland Road, before, during and after rebuilding work which took place in 1935.

Rosarium 'Bed of Roses', No 40 Sunderland Road with the County Hotel visible on the right. It was so named by the builder T.B. Carr because it had a bed of roses in the garden. *Opposite page, top*: The dismantling and rebuilding of Rosarium in 1935. *Bottom*: The rebuilt Rosarium complete with horse trough outside. Ethel Ord, who lived in the house, recalls:

'When I was very young the council decided to transfer Westoe Fountain from the area at the top of Imeary Street to just outside our front door to allow them to widen the road junction at Westoe. The Council did not consult my father about it at all and suddenly it was there outside our front door. While it might look picturesque on old photographs it was actually a great source of aggravation as of course we soon had horses and their associated dirt outside as well and there were children paying in it, splashing water about. After some time, there was a court case and the fountain was carted off to the Corporation Yard. A local character I can recall being around was a man who lived in Dean Road called Dirty Dan. He had a barrow and went around all the builders collecting their wood chipping which he would make into bundles and sell them to people as sticks to light their coal fires with. He also collected things and one day he knocked at our front door and my father gave him a coat which my mother took out to him. I was in one of our upstairs rooms at the time and remember her coming back upstairs with a surprised expression on her face saying, "You'll never guess, he wants the trousers as well!" In 1935 our house was pulled down and rebuilt in its own garden. What had happened was that someone wanted to build a garage in our garden. My father was agreeable, but this was a commercial garage with petrol pumps and workshops and our next door neighbour objected to the idea. The solution was to move our house and let the garage be built on the old site. It may sound like a drastic thing to do but it kept everybody happy. The garage itself is gone now, our new house has outlasted it, but it did stand next to the County public house for a great many years.'

Rosarium 1935

"ROSARIUM"
40, SUNDERLAND RD
SOUTH SHIELDS

A postcard view of Westoe Village, *circa* 1900. Around a hundred years later this view is little changed.

Members of St Stephen's Bowling Club at the Readhead Park, 1933.

Members of the Women's National Liberal Club at Westoe Village, 1938.

Employees of
Redhead and Sons
in the funeral
procession of Sir
James Readhead,
the head of the
firm, on the journey
to Harton cemetery.
The backdrop is
Westoe Village.

*Above*: George Foster, aged two years eight months, at Westoe Cricket Ground, August Bank Holiday Monday, 1962. *Below*: George with his parents, Jim and Irene Foster.

Passengers being dropped off from a trolleybus in Dean Road.

Dean Road from Chichester. Being both a tramway junction and very near Dean Road depot this was a logical place for tram crew changes to take place, one seems to be in progress in this *circa* 1910 image. Stagecoach South Shields drivers still use this point for the same reasons, although its unlikely many of them will be able to stroll across the road in the same manner this crew seems to be doing. Interestingly the caption to this photograph gives the location as Meldon Terrace, Tyne Dock.

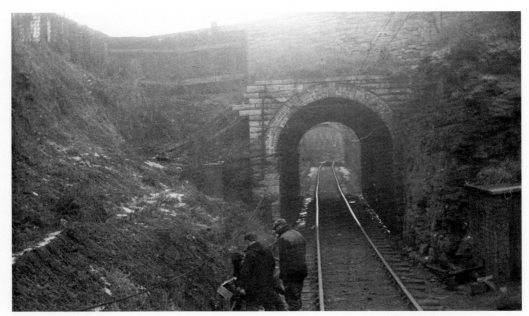

We suspect few people will have any idea of where this location is even though almost all Shields people will have passed over this arch countless times in their lives. The location is the former Harton Coal Company and later NCB railway passing under Laygate Lane at Chichester. The date is early 1960s. This is now the site of Chichester Metro Station with the camera being positioned near the north end of the Newcastle bound platform.

Construction work underway on Chichester Metro Station. We believe this is around 1981. The view is towards South Shields and the remains of the bridge can just be made out towards the left of the picture.

Looking down Laygate Lane towards Chichester, *circa* 1960. The stone wall to the right is the same one that is visible on top of the arch on the opposite page.

Looking down Laygate Lane from roughly the same position but around twenty years on. The old Laygate School building has been replaced and the again Metro construction work is very visible.

Two views of traction engines engaged in agricultural work around 1910. The location of the top image at least, and in all probability both, is known to be at Red House Farm Harton.

Councillor James Curbison. While researching this book we came across several references to Councillor Curbison. He seems to have been a very principled man and a great defender of the town's less privileged citizens. In one debate, after Curbison refused appeals by the Mayor to give way and sit down, the Mayor summoned a police constable to the chamber to eject him. Pandemonium and loud booing broke out in the public gallery, drowning the Mayor's appeal for calm and, following a scuffle involving other councillors, Curbison was escorted out of the Town Hall. Curbison was himself voted Mayor of the town a short while later. There were some suggestions that he was ideally suited to a life in the clergy.

Albert Rose, aged around 18, outside No 46 Greens Place, *circa* 1934. He worked for the T.W. Urwin Trawler Company. We believe that Greens Place is named after Mr Robert Green who resided in a large house near Commercial Road and owned much of the land in the area.

'The Little Dustpan', 16 and 17 Cuthbert Street, *circa* 1903. Established around 1885 by a Mr John Strother, the nature of its business was as a wholesale and retail ironmonger and brush factor. Cuthbert Street is believed to be named after the owner of a brickworks near to Eldon Street, which stood on land owned by the Green family.

Margaret Miller (née Ramshaw) with her son Richard outside 285 Taylor Street. In the background is Wilkinson's shop in Gilbert Street. The date is shortly before World War Two. Taylor Street was named after foundry owner Charles Taylor.

Vaux's off licence at 121 Dale Street.

# James Grisdale, 47=48, Green Street.
## . . and Lawson Street.

HAS THE LARGEST AND CHEAPEST SELECTION OF

## Ladies' and Children's Millinery.

### Infants' Millinery a Speciality.

Corsets, Underclothing, Ribbons, Gloves, Lace, Scarfs, Umbrellas, Trimmings, &c.

Dress Goods, Draperies, Flannels, Blankets, Sheets, Quilts, Lace Curtains, Canvas, &c.

## The Leading Gent's Outfitter.

GENT'S WHITE SHIRTS, PRINT SHIRTS, WOOL SHIRTS, &c.

GENT'S COLLARS, TIES, CUFFS, BRACES, STUDS, &c.

ALL GOODS AT POPULAR PRICES.

★ ★ ★ ★ ★

# 47=48, GREEN STREET, SOUTH SHIELDS.

*TRADING STAMPS ON ALL PURCHASES.*

An advertisement for James Grisdale Gent's Outfitter, Green Street, *circa* 1902.

Wesley Chapel and Schools, Frederick Street. Built in the 1880s in the Queen Ann Style at a cost of £4,292 for the site and building. It closed in 1972.

Vaux's off license at 47 Frederick Street.

*Above and below*: The Interior of the La Strada Night Club. The club opened its doors in December 1961. Its proprietor was twenty-five-year-old Stanford Goudie. Although the exterior was an unremarkable brick building, for the interior Goudie had apparently visited dozens of other clubs in England and the continent incorporating the aspects he liked into his own design. The Spanish influence downstairs included a bull's head and matador's cape, hat and swords in one room while the main upstairs room had a German tavern theme complete with a wild boars head on the wall. A £400 roulette table was flown in from Paris and was housed in a room hung with red crushed velvet curtains called the Monte Carlo room. The architect was local, a Mr C. Luke who also supervised the building work. The new club was to have several firm policies. Stanford Goudie had definite views on membership and members conduct. 'There is no boy meets girl element to our club. Many of the members are seafarers and we want this to be a place where the wives can come for a good evening when their husbands are at sea. If a couple is seen necking then they are asked very politely to cease. We've never had any trouble about that policy.'

Joyce Carlson recalls: 'All guests had to wear evening dress. Women wore long sometimes strapless evening gowns, men wore evening suits with bow ties, just as I had seen in the casinos in Monte Carlo.'

Members had to be over 21, although most seemed to be between 30 and 60. Perhaps to forestall concerns over members gambling away their pay-packets, Goudie remarked that no one would lose a packet at La Strada as the stakes would be controlled by a croupier. Early in 1963 the club was employing forty two staff and there were three and a half thousand members on the books with another two thousand on the waiting list. Cabaret was provided by first class performers.

Joyce Carlson also recalls: 'The club was an instant success with me. I wasn't interested in the gambling it was the cabaret that attracted me and the way the interior reminded me of Toulouse Lautrec's painting, 'At the Moulon Rouge.' Years later, in 1981, I used the club as a basis for a transcription of Lautrec's painting (*below*). At the table in the foreground are left Charles Carlson, Lorna Abbott, John Carlson and two unknown characters from Lautrec's painting. Standing centre in the background is Barney the manager. The small group of three people immediately in front of him is left to right, Mary Peterson, Mary Pearson and myself. The main group at the table is balanced by a young woman's face eerily reflected by a green yellow light from above. Pauline Abbot, daughter of Lorna Abbot, posed for this character.'

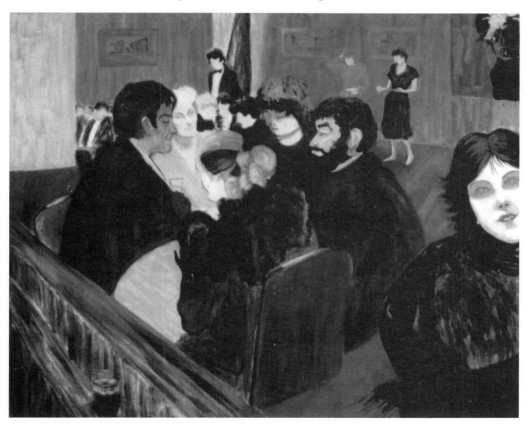

St Hilda Colliery, 1892. At this point the Harton Coal Company was embarking on a vigorous period of modernisation and electrification.

George May, Mining Engineer for the Harton Collieries, 1872-1902 and President of the North of England Institute of Mining and Mechanical Engineers, 1896-1898.

A telegraph aerial supplied by Thomas W. MacNay and Co, Royal Exchange, Middlesborough, in a colliery siding at one of the HCC's Collieries.

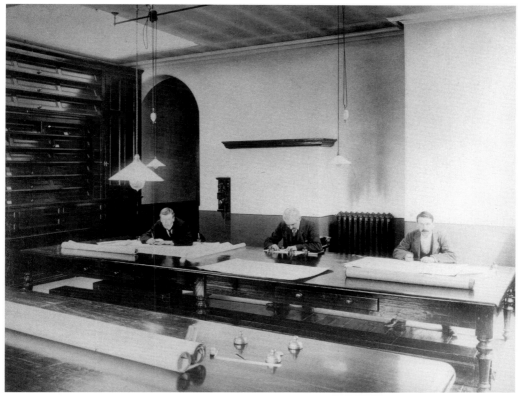

What appears to be the drawing office of the HCC. Weights for holding plans flat can be seen on the desk.

The lobby of the Harton Coal Companies Offices, 1890.

St Hilda sidings some time after the Harton Coal Company was nationalised to become part of the National Coal Board on 1st January 1947. The bridge to the right, which carried Claypath Lane over the HCC's lines, is visible to rear and the former St Hilda engine shed stands at the right of it. Electric locomotive E9, now on the Tanfield Railway is to the front. This image may have been taken from the viaduct pictured below.

Another view of Claypath Lane Bridge this time looking north. Part of the gas works is visible between the bridge supports. This is one of a series of surveyors' photographs taken in the late 1950s prior to rebuilding work in the area.

In 1872 South Shields was linked to Newcastle via Jarrow by the North Eastern Railway. Part of the route ran across this viaduct which bisected the HCC's land around St Hilda Colliery. The viaduct arches were effectively colonised by the colliery, but when this image was taken around 1960 they seemed to be falling into disuse. The viaduct became redundant in 1981 and was demolished shortly afterwards. In the foreground an inspection train consisting of a land rover on a flat wagon being drawn by the National Coal Board's tower car makes its way from Westoe Colliery towards the High Staiths near Commercial Road.

The Harton Coal Company's yard at Waterloo Vale.

The Union British School at Waterloo Vale. We believe this was the first undenominational school opened in the Borough.

Messrs Thomas Coulson and Son, Dealers in Plate Crown and Sheet Glass, 18 Barrington Street, *circa* 1900. The business was started in 1885 by Thomas Coulson senior.

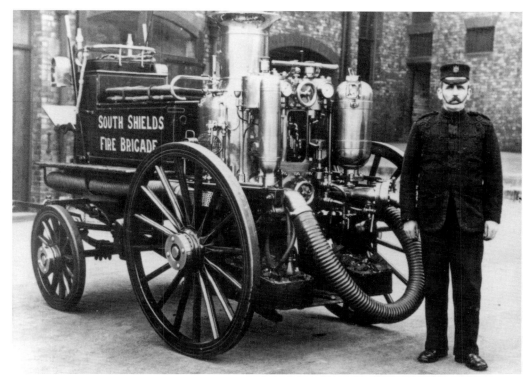

A fireman and fire engine at the back of Kepple Street Station.

*Right*: a house in Chapter Row, *circa* 1900, that was once home to some of the town's Methodist Ministers. *Far right*: Chapter Row Methodist Chapel. The ground cost the church £300 and the building itself £3,000. The authors believe that when it was built in 1807/8, the timber used in its construction was floated up the Mill Dam Gut. The building was said

to be unremarkable but a very solid piece of workmanship. It was opened on 21st February 1809 by the Rev Isaacs. There was accommodation for 1700 worshippers and at that time it was said to be the largest place of worship in the town.

A staff outing from John Chipchase and Co, Wine and Spirits Merchants. We believe this firm was located around the Mill Dam area.

Gaddes, Confectioner and Tobacconist at the Mill Dam. The shop is now part of The Steamboat public house with the woodwork outside pretty much untouched.

The Locomotive public house at the Mill Dam.

The former Ferry Tavern, River Drive.

The back lane between Grace Street and Ivy Street. This and the two images opposite, of proposed slum clearance areas, were taken by the South Shields photographer James Henry Cleet for South Shields Corporation in the early 1930s. Very clear prints of these and many other photographs of similar areas in the town are held in various archives. Almost all show very precisely streets, patches of ground or groups of buildings with very few have landmarks that are standing today. Most seem to have been taken on damp days perhaps to highlight the squalid nature of many areas of the town. When first viewing them today it's possible in spite of Cleet's intentions to perceive a sort of old world charm about these images of close knit communities, corner shops and gas lights. Then after a few minutes of looking at photograph after photograph a sense of decay creeps in and it's easy to imagine the despair generated by life in these areas coupled with prolonged periods of unemployment. There would be happy times, but it's worth trying to mentally picture how fantastically sturdy and modern the new Cleadon Park housing estate must have seemed to the people who lived here and remembering that some of these buildings were still standing until after the Second World War. There are of course still problem areas in Shields, but hopefully the town will never see slums on this scale again.

*Above*: 18-28 Woodbine street. *Below*: A back yard in John Street.

The Mile End Road premises of John Christie and Sons, Slaters and Slate
Merchants opposite Mile End Road Railway Station. The business began in
1867 from a yard in Claypath Lane moving to Ocean Road some years after, as
building work increased in that area. In 1899 they were obliged to sell the yard
when the Corporation obtained Parliamentary Powers for public street
improvements. The company held contracts with the Cemetery Chapels, County
Hotel, Britannia Inn, Victoria Hall and Westoe Road School.

The premises of
William Johnson,
Bill Poster and
Advertising
Contractor, (back)
Mile End Road,
*circa* 1901. As well
as Shields, the
company covered
East Jarrow and
Boldon Colliery
areas.

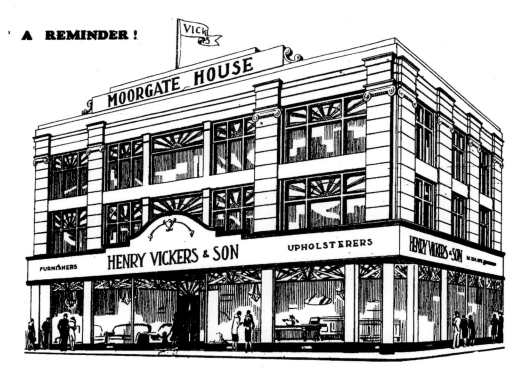

An illustration taken from an advertisement for Henry Vickers and Son, Upholsterers in Mile End Road, *circa* 1930. We believe the building was later occupied by Smiths Upholsterers.

A Corporation Trolleybus in Mile End Road, *circa* 1959.

Two of Cleet's slum clearance photographs for South Shields Corporation taken around 1935. Here they show conditions on the Lawe Top in Wellington Street.

A group of young people at the Lawe Top.

At the Lawe Top around 1960. Pictured are William Parker Junior, Albert Parker and William Parker Senior. Also visible is some of the very modern council housing which replaced some of the slum housing Cleet was photographing.

In the run up to the 2001 General Election there were allegations that sitting Labour members of Parliament were 'suddenly' resigning to allow 'outsiders' or 'favoured new boys' to be parachuted into safe Parliamentary seats such as South Shields with local party members being given no say in candidates and little effective choice to question them before a vote took place. Parts of this book were being put together as the election took place and whatever our thoughts on the matter were, we were slightly amused to find this letter to the *Gazette* about the South Shields Ward election from about a century ago suggesting parachuted candidates and carefully worded protests against them are nothing new:

'Sir,_ I at one time thought that the election of a Councillor for South Shields ward was going to attract so little attention as not even to produce one letter in your widely read paper. I have nothing to say against Mr Grunhut as a gentleman, but I think him totally unfit to represent South Shields Ward in the Council. What does he know about South Shields Ward and what does South Shields Ward know about him? I quite agree with the sentiment that the councillors ought to let the burgesses choose candidates themselves. It is scarcely a dignified procedure to choose men in back parlours of inns, and then push then before the ratepayers for their suffrages. I am not sure that this has been done in the case of Mr Grunhut, but it is evidently a party move, and his candidature is being conducted as such. It is even being carried out on religious grounds. There is quite a stir among a few Roman Catholics in the ward. I heard Mr Grunhut paid for a stained glass window in their chapel. Well I like to see people grateful but, but it is hardly the right thing for which to make a man a Town Councillor. In the meeting held to introduce Mr Grunhut to the public – he being a perfect stranger to the Shields Ward – the principal speakers told us what a nice, generous, gentleman Mr Grunhut is. I for one don't doubt it. But a man may be generous, but very unfit for a town councillor. There was not one claim put forwards at the meeting for which the ratepayers should vote for Mr Grunhut except that he is a very nice gentleman. Even Councillor Drake could say nothing in his favour – he only encouraged a vote of thanks to the chairman. I think Mr Smith has the best claim to the suffrages of the ratepayers. He has been resident in our ward for a long time, he is an employer of labour and is as much a gentleman as Mr Grunhut; and from his business habits much better fitted to represent us in the Council. Therefor I trust that the ratepayers will vote not from mere acquaintance, or from generous gifts, but in order to send a man to the council who is known and whose business habits will fit him for the duties he is to discharge.

Yours A. Burgess.

Bearing Street Church in the
course of construction in 1904
and the architect's design. It
was the last architectural work
of or Mr T.A. Page who also
designed Wesley and West
Harton Churches. His son,
James Page, carried the work to
completion.

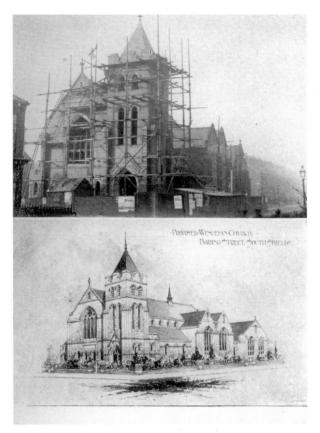

A Corporation trolleybus running up to the terminus at the Lawe Top, *circa*
1959.

Ships at anchor near the Groyne, *circa* 1890.

A ship aground on the pier.

TYNEMOUTH FROM NORTH MARINE PARK, SOUTH SHIELDS.

Tugs in the Tyne off the Groyne, *circa* 1912.

Crewmembers aboard a Tyne fishing boat, *circa* 1960.

French Onion Men,
Francoise Salaun, Jean Marie
Quere and his brother,
Pierre, in Shields, 1958.

Jacqueline Rouse recalls: 'I was born in 1920, my parents had been married in 1919. My mother Blanch Folliot was French. My father William Millar was a shipping butcher for Peterson's the shipping suppliers. I remember the French Onion Men coming over from Brittany and cycling around Shields. On talking to some of them my father suggested they knock at our door to speak with my mother not realising that as they were from Brittany they spoke a completely different type of French to her. Nevertheless over the years our house became a place where the French Onion men would call in for a chat and a cup of tea or coffee when they had finished their rounds. I remember they would knock at people's doors and when the door was answered they would hold up a string of onions saying, "Onions a shilling a bunch and a penny for myself."

My husband had a glass eye and before he went out he would stand it in a saucer of water on the table. One day, just as he was about to go, the dog lapped up the water along with the eye. I shouted, "The dog's got your eye in her mouth, get her."

But he hissed at me, "Don't shout at her or she'll crunch it."

Thankfully we were able to prize it out of her mouth then wash it before he popped it back into its socket.

When I was landlady at the Royal Hotel in Hudson Street, Tyne Dock a man who was a well known character called 'Tot' Wright used to come in. He was a lovely singer and he had an audition to go on TV. Jack Leighton, who I think ran the 21 Club at Tyne Dock lent him a lovely dress suit with silk lapels for his appearance. I don't know how that went but a few days later he came into the royal wearing the suit and, of course as always, his Wellington's. The suit was all marked with paint as he had been decorating the 21 Club. I said, "Tot, you've ruined that suit. Why have you been wearing it at work?"

He said, "Well I had nothing else to put on!" He was a likeable person but somehow he didn't seem to care about things like that. He went everywhere wearing his big Wellies, including dances and his various club appearances as a singer.

People have asked me why I went into the pub game and I always reply it was because my husband went away to sea for two years at a time and the pub life gave me great company and plenty of laughs.'

The Marine Park and Bandstand, *circa* 1912.

The Lime kilns at Marsden, *circa* 1960. The kilns are now a listed structure although it seems uncertain when any kind of restoration work will take place on them.

Looking North from Trow Rocks, South Shields.

The North Sands looking from Trow Rocks. Bathing machines were placed on the South Sands as early as 1859 and a portion of the sands were set aside for ladies. The Town Improvement Bill of 1896 as originally introduced by the Corporation sought powers to take over, control and develop the fine sands on the Foreshore and to prevent their abuse. During the progress of the bill through Parliament, the Harton Coal Company surrendered their leasehold of some 62 acres of land between Trow Rocks and the South Park in return for concessions from the Corporation on the construction and extension of their railways in the Borough.

Elizabeth Ramshaw and friend on the Littlehaven beach in the late 1930s. The family had a tent on the beach for the whole of the summer season.

Trow Rocks, *circa* 1900.

Frenchman's Bay, *circa* 1900.

A Corporation Trolleybus swings past the Marsden Inn. The Marsden Inn is one of those Shields buildings that everyone knows, but few seem to know very much about. It was designed in Mock Tudor style by Messrs T.A. Page, Son and Bradbury, South Shields and constructed by Mr George Henderson of East Boldon and Sunderland. The inn hardly opened in the best of circumstances, the official ceremony took place early in December 1939 as war, sandbags and conscription were looming large in many peoples lives. An advertising feature covering the opening made the sombre comment that the building combined 'comfort, hygiene, luxury and elegance to offer hospitality to all in search of that democratic atmosphere which is the Britons most treasured possession.' We believe the plaster heraldic devices on the exterior walls have no special significance. The first floor included a public dining room and ten bedrooms described as 'absolutely the last word in modernity.' The interior decoration and styling was carried out by W.L. Swann and Co of South Shields. The lounge was fitted with old time oak rafters supported by carved herds. There was an old wiped ivory effect on the ceiling while the walls were panelled in a rich tone of oak. A.J. Wares Ltd, South Shields, carried out the fireplaces, hardware and electrical instillation. Every main entrance hall was fitted with a large wrought iron chandelier with light switch plates in antique iron. The outside bell pulls were wrought iron, although they actually operated electric bells. At the time of writing this book, the travel business is facing up to the problems caused by the destruction of the World Trade Centre in New York and we wonder who exactly took advantage of the Marsden Inn's opulence during the years of World War Two. We don't know, although as many of the surrounding housing estates were yet to be built we assume its upper rooms would have given a commanding view of much of the area including the coast. Perhaps this was taken advantage of by members of the Home Guard.

Whitburn Colliery, 1901. Later rows of housing would be built in the empty fields,. Today the houses remain and the colliery site is grassed over and landscaped. In the 1960s a film staring Patrick McGoohan was made around this area. Apparently the script required miners to cross the road to the pit head baths. But by this time an overhead walkway linked pit and baths and the NCB forbid working miners crossing at road level. Hence off duty miners had to be hired, at equity rates we hope, to cross the road.

The winding engines for Whitburn Colliery, No 2 Pit erected in 1897.

Whitburn Colliery. Apparently the HCC had a reputation for employing 'church like' architecture and glimpses of that are visible here.

The fire clay brickworks at Whitburn.

Cleadon Park veterans in the shelter by the bowling green in the early 1960s.

Corporation Trolleybus No 254 at the Nook, *circa* 1958. Their electric motors gave trolleybuses very fast acceleration. Apparently as they pulled away from stops, the wheels would spin so fast that they caused older road surfaces to melt.

Souter Point Lighthouse. The lighthouse was constructed in 1871 to prevent wrecks on Whitburn Steel and actually stands at Lizard Point. The Souter name was taken because a Lizard Point Lighthouse already existed in Cornwall. In later years the lighthouse was granted offshore status because dust blowing in from Marsden Quarry made the keeper's cottages unsuitable for families and the lighthouse began to be worked on the shift system. The lighthouse closed in 1988 and the Grade Two Listed Building was soon acquired by the National Trust.

# PEOPLE OF
# SOUTH SHIELDS

A group of coal wagons and their drivers at the Harton Coal Company's depot at Waterloo Vale.

These two images are a something of a mystery. They are embossed with the stamp of a South Shields photographer and we believe they are taken in the town but why this crowd is gathered is unclear. They are pretty much snapshots rather than the more usual posed shots of the time although they could show the anticipation and arrival of a group of dignitaries at a building site. The initials C.A. just visible on the signs could be of Christian Association and this might be the laying of the foundation stone at the YMCA, Fowler Street.

The corner shop in Baring Street owned by Granny Watts (who is standing at the back) in the early 1900s. In front of her, with ribbons in her hair, is her daughter, Jessie. To the right is Jessie's sister, Margaret.

Members of Westoe Rugby team in 1938. The match was Westoe v North Durham in the final of the Senior Cup at Ashbrooke, Sunderland.

South Shields Borough Police FC in the 1930s. Back row: A. Green, G. Falkingham, W. Beattie, E. Browning, F. Kennedy, W. Hoggan. Front row: T. Barkel (Secretary), W. Driver, W. Storey (Captain), T. Little, W. Milne. Seated on the ground: J. Mordue and

S. Shepperd. The team, who played only on Wednesdays, contributed large sums to charity. They were members of the Northern Police League and played in a number of local charity competitions. In the 1935-36 season they were runners-up for the Ingham Infirmary Bowl and South Shields Shoeless Children's Cup.

South Shields Middle Docks FC in the 1930s. Back row: S. Camillieri (Trainer), W. Davidson, J. Spence, J. Rowe, R. Longmore, G. Guyan (Captain), E. Sarginson, G. Gray (Secretary). Front row: Dr N. Franks, M. Bainbridge, R. Gidney, S. Nichols, A. Common. At this time they were members of the South Tyne Alliance and were League Champions in the 1935-36 season.

South Shields Adelaide FC in the 1930s. Back row: C. Dew (Trainer), Westal, A. Wetherson, T. Sibson, J. McGlasham (Captain), J. Murray, J. Dew, W. Potts (Secretary). Front row: J. Frazer, M. Beck, D. Currie, T. Wilson, A. Boyack.

Members of the Seamen's Minority Movement at the Mill Dam during the signing on of the crew of the *Goolistan*, *circa* 1930.

Local people taking part in a 1920s carnival. Elizabeth Ramshaw is holding the mace. The group is posed in the Lytton Street/Taylor Street backlane.

Members of the local Royal Observer Corps crew beside the observation post E4 – Easy Fowler, 'the best post on the coast' – with the pennant and cup won in a 30 Group (Durham) competition. The date is early 1950s. The post was located in a flower bed in the West park. Back row: Len Cook, Walter Morley, John Bond, Lewie Thompson, George Hunter. Front row: Arthur Montgomery, Marmie Wetherell, Chief Observer, John Johnson.

A group of South Shields pilots ready to depart on an charabanc trip.

# The Poor Bairns' Gala

In the 19th century, the town's people would hold galas for the children from the area's poorer families. The following is drawn from a *Shields Gazette* report, *circa* 1900.

Yesterday, a Poor Bairns' Gala was held at South Shields. The gathering was the result of a committee of benevolent ladies and gentlemen, whose excertations on behalf of the poor children of the Borough have been recorded in the *Gazette* from time to time. With the assistance of the teachers of the various schools, the poorer children were selected for the 'outing' and today over two thousand of them assembled in the Market Place. They had previously gathered in their respective schools, and from thence marched to the rendezvous under the guidance of the marshals and their assistants. The destination of the happy army of youngsters was a spacious field at the Bent House Farm, the use of which was kindly granted for the occasion by Mr Peacock. Long before the time appointed for the assembling of the children, 2.30pm, large numbers of people gathered in the Market Place and adjacent streets. The Town Hall steps were crowded with spectators and both sides of King Street were lined with people. The children began to arrive about two o'clock and shortly afterwards the marshals, carrying coloured flags, put in an appearance. The marshals took up positions in the Market Place, and the children who had received the committee's invitation to the gala at once began to range themselves under their respective banners, tickets being their passports. Each child carried his or her own jug or can for the tea provided. Among the large number of children assembled were some who had not received tickets and consequently could not join the ranks of their more fortunate brethren. In such instances the looks of disappointment were touching to the extreme. In the majority of cases the children were decently dressed, but there were many who were shoeless and in rags. All looked the picture of happiness, however. The weather was favourable, though not bright but sufficiently promising for venturing to the field. Supporting the marshals were a large number of ladies and gentlemen wearing rosettes of the same colour as the standard under which they marched, and the children wore their tickets which were coloured by section, pinned to their clothes. The children were arranged in lines two deep across the Market Place, some of the divisions reaching from pavement to pavement.

A few minutes after half past two o'clock the Workhouse Band, which had taken up a position near the Town Hall and facing King Street, struck up a lively march and the procession moved on, the children marching four deep, with their little arms linked or holding each other by the hands. Behind the third section came the St Jude's Drum and File Band, and then followed by two other divisions. Cart and carriage traffic was delayed for the time being, and within a quarter of an hour of the start of the procession, the last of the children had left the Market Place. The Wellesly Band was not present, owing, we were informed, to the illness of some of the little musicians. The scenes en route – King Street, Ocean Road, Seafield Terrace, Sea View Terrace, and Salisbury Place – were thronged with spectators and almost every window was occupied. The children marched orderly and silently, and appeared to thoroughly enjoy the march. In addition to the marshal's flags, there were a few banners. The sight of so many poor children marching through busy thoroughfares was somewhat pathetic, and many were the sympathetic remarks of the onlookers. On the other hand, a glance at the kindly guides walking by the side of the children had a cheering effect, showing as it did that the link between the poor and those more favourably situated in life remains unbroken.

Entering the field in double line the children were marched to spaces enclosed by stakes bearing flags of the same colour as the tickets attached to the children's dresses. The boys having been ranged at one end of the enclosure, and the girls upon the other the whole were ordered to sit upon the grass , and the attendants at once proceeded to dispense the good things, each child being allowed a pint of tea and a large sandwich. They were placed in hampers in different parts of the field, and thus all the confusion which arises through having the victuals in the centre tent was avoided. There was a great amount of excitement and stir but no hitch occurred in the carrying out of the arrangements. To describe the scene which followed the dispensation of the buns and tea is almost an impossibility. The children 'fell to' with remarkable vigour and in many cases, and especially in the boys' section, the cakes disappeared 'like winking'. Little ceremony was observed. So soon was one 'course' was completed, the young Olivers sung out for more, and the teachers and others had a lively half hour of it. At length all seemed satisfied and the order was given to 'stand to attention'. This was obeyed with great alacrity for the Punch and Judy show had been placed in position and certain mysterious noises from the interior suggested that the celebrated 'razor and sausage quarrel' was about to begin. The show being situated upon a rising part of the ground, the children were conveniently placed upon the opposite bank, the whole, when crowded, had the appearance of an amphitheatre. In addition grotesque balloons were despatched at short intervals. Punch's family quarrel having been concluded, the children formed themselves into 'kissing rings' or chose partners for 'Sally Walker'. The sports concluded at six o'clock when each child was presented with a spice bun. There is not doubt that the present fete will live long in the memories of those waifs, and form the subject of numerous chats amongst them in years to come.

The following ladies generously undertook to supply tea to a part of the children: Mrs Morgan 400; Mrs Henderson 400; Mrs Donaldson 200; Mrs Hutchinson 200; and Mrs Winter 100. Messrs A. and A. Johnson confectioners gave 200 buns as their contribution to the treat. The remaining 900 children were provided for by Mr Henderson, confectioner, Fowler Street on Tender. In the evening, a number of the committee were entertained to supper at the Criterion Hotel, Ocean Road by the manageress, Mrs Morgan.

A portrait group of three South Shields Victorian ladies in 1899. They are from left to right: Jane Hunter, Mrs Keen and her daughter Lilly. Jane Hunter was a dressmaker.

The wedding day of Foster Bell Ryan and Mary D'or Ryan (née Porter) at St Michael's Church, South Shields, 10th June 1939. Back row: Charlie (Best Man), Groom, Bride, Amy Porter (Chief Bridesmaid) and Roland Porter (the Bride's brother who gave her away). Front row: Bill Porter (Page Boy), Jean Porter and Sheila Dickinson (Bridesmaid).

*Right*: Mary D'or Porter in Byron Street, 1939.

*Far right*: Foster Bell Ryan in 1935.

Valerie Dunmore (née Clemens) aged 15 in 1961 outside her house in Hylton Avenue during her first week at work. She recalls: 'I was born in Saville Street in 1946 in my Grandmother's house. My Grandmother had six girls and one son. I had a lot of cousins so had lots of playmates to play with around the streets. My Grandmother's house had cellars and we used to play with gas masks and swords which we found down there, we had a great time. There was a dentist's repair shop in Saville Street and we would stand for ages at the shop window entranced by the rows of false teeth on display which were in for repair. At Easter we would go to local Salvation Army hall and get what at the time seemed to be a huge orange. When I was fifteen I worked for Smith's Furnishing Company in the office at 2A King Street which is now a café. It was a poorly paid job but I have

lovely memories of it. We were like a family. I was office junior and some older girls were bookkeepers. The building had three floors. If you stood on the top floor you could see down onto the lower floors. There were typewriters tapping away all day. My job was to file people's documents and arrears, and go to the post office for stamps. A lady cleaner called Cathy used to sing all day and make the tea. We had good tea breaks and an hour and a half for lunch. When a woman got married it was automatic that she left her job. It was the rule in those days and quite a lot of women came and went. If a widow with children applied she would be taken on as she had responsibilities. We had a boss called Mr Michie. Near five o'clock he would look at his watch and we all stood up to attention and waited for the signal from him. Then right on five he would nod his head and all the girls would clash down the shutters of the bookkeeping cabinets. It was time to go home. We would take broken typewriters and adding machines to a gentleman, Ellis Bowden, who had premises in King Street. He was very polite and had white hair, fair complexion and rosy cheeks.

South Shields postman, Dennis
Boad, in Kepple Street, *circa* 1990.

Beryl, wife of Dennis Boad, with a
friend, *circa* 1960.

South Shields Corporation Tram No 50 at the Pier Head.

## The People's History

To receive a catalogue of our latest titles send a large SAE to:

The People's History
Suite 1
Byron House
Seaham Grange Business Park
Seaham
County Durham
SR7 0PY